LIGHT AND SOUND

SOUND

by Michael Dahl

Raintree is an imprint of Capstone Global Library Limited, a company incorporated in England and Wales having its registered office at 264 Banbury Road, Oxford, OX2 7DY – Registered company number: 6695582

www.raintree.co.uk
myorders@raintree.co.uk

Copyright © Capstone Global Library Limited 2022

The moral rights of the proprietor have been asserted. All rights reserved. No part of this publication may be reproduced in any form or by any means (including photocopying or storing it in any medium by electronic means and whether or not transiently or incidentally to some other use of this publication) without the written permission of the copyright owner, except in accordance with the provisions of the Copyright, Designs and Patents Act 1988 or under the terms of a licence issued by the Copyright Licensing Agency, 5th Floor, Shackleton House, 4 Battle Bridge Lane, London, SE1 2HX (www.cla.co.uk). Applications for the copyright owner's written permission should be addressed to the publisher.

ISBN 978 1 3982 0418 8 (hardback)
ISBN 978 1 3982 0419 5 (paperback)

Image Credits
Capstone Studio: Karon Dubke, 20; Shutterstock: Andrea Danti, 8, Cris Matei, 11, Dean Drobot, 14, Firefighter Montreal, 19, gritsalak karalak, CONTRIBUTOR, 7, ilusmedical, 9, Paul Reeves Photography, 13, Rudm 17, Sergey Novikov, 5, Steve Byland, Cover, STILLFX, 12
Design Elements
Capstone; Shutterstock: Miloje, Ursa Major

Editorial Credits
Editor: Michelle Parkin; Designer: Ted Williams; Media Researcher: Jo Miller; Production Specialist: Laura Manthe

All internet sites appearing in back matter were available and accurate when this book was sent to press.

British Library Cataloguing in Publication Data
A full catalogue record for this book is available from the British Library.

Printed and bound in India

CONTENTS

SOUND 4

MOVING THE AIR 6

YOUR EAR 8

SOUND MESSAGES 10

PITCH 12

ECHO 14

SOUND ALL AROUND 18

MAKE MUSICAL SOUND WAVES 20

    GLOSSARY 22

    FIND OUT MORE 23

    INDEX 24

Words in **bold** are in the glossary.

SOUND

Have you ever been to the beach? Have you watched the **waves** move through the water? The waves move all around.

There are other types of waves that you cannot see. These waves are all around us. They move through the air. They are called sound waves. Sound waves help our ears to hear.

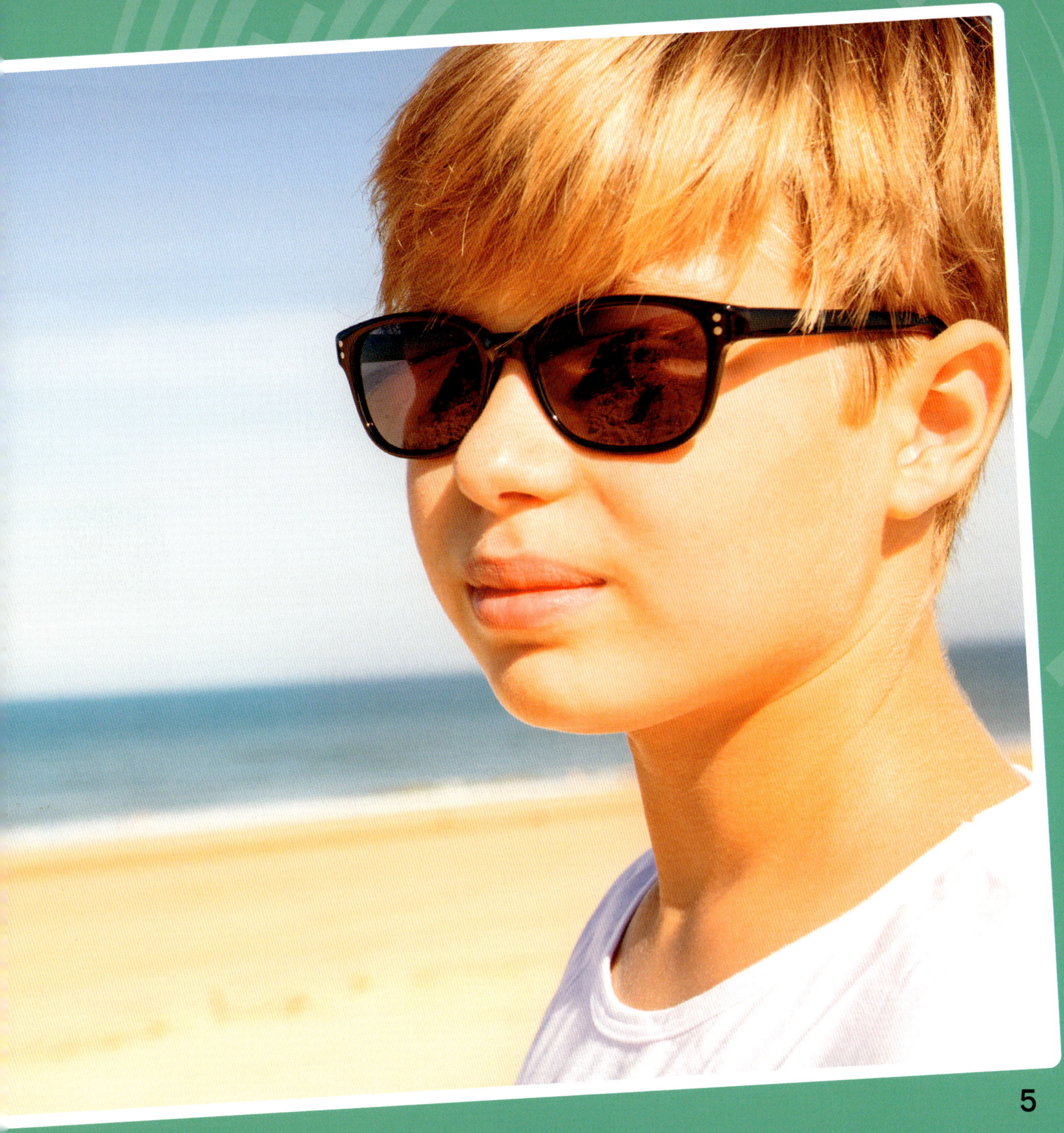

MOVING THE AIR

Sound waves are made by moving air. Ask a friend to hold a rubber band. Tell your friend to hold the ends tight. Pull the middle of the rubber band and let it go!

Watch how the rubber band moves back and forth. The moving band is **vibrating**. The vibrations move the air around it. Can you hear the sound it makes?

7

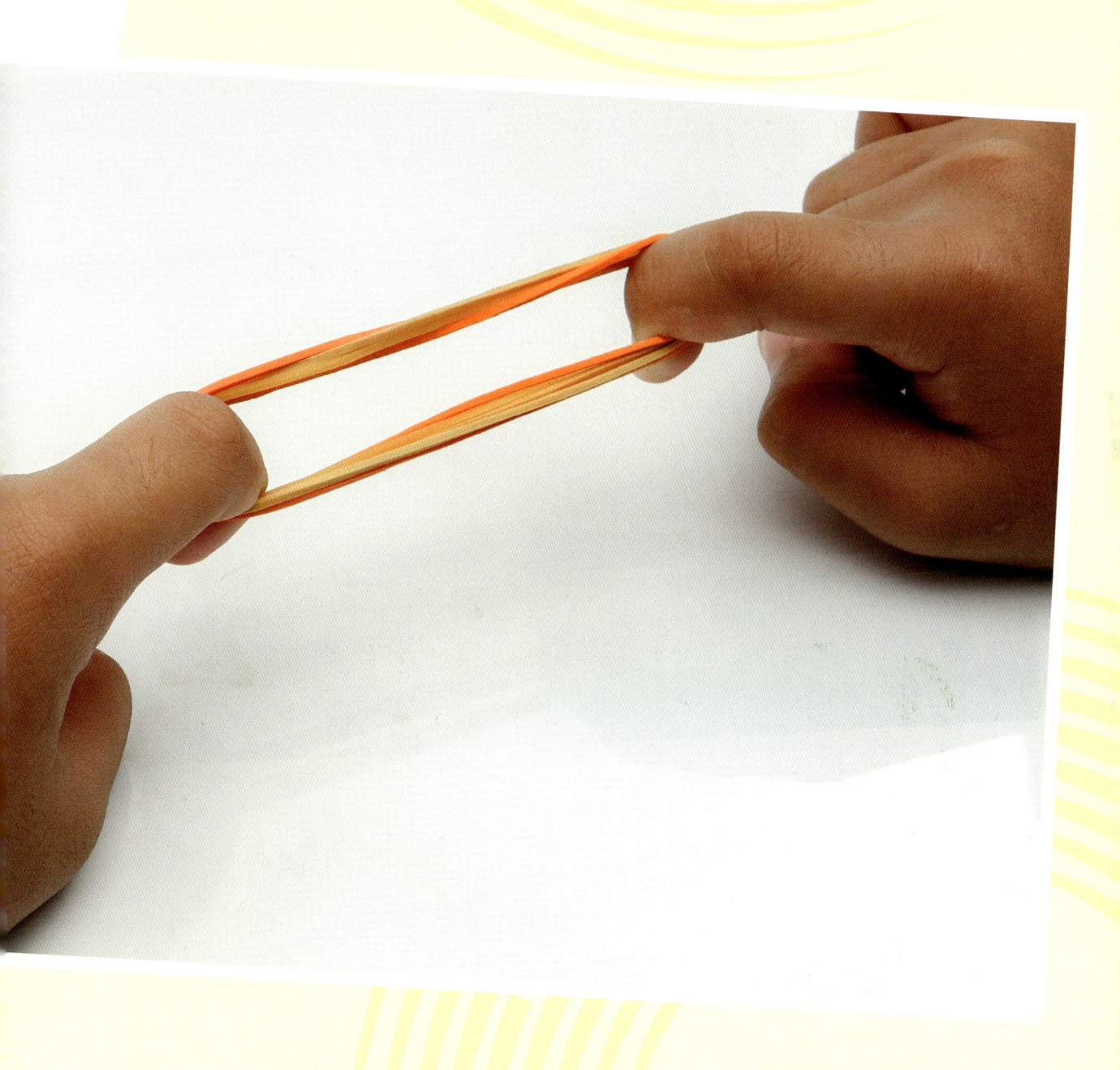

YOUR EAR

You cannot see a sound wave. You can only hear it. When the sound wave reaches your ear, it goes inside.

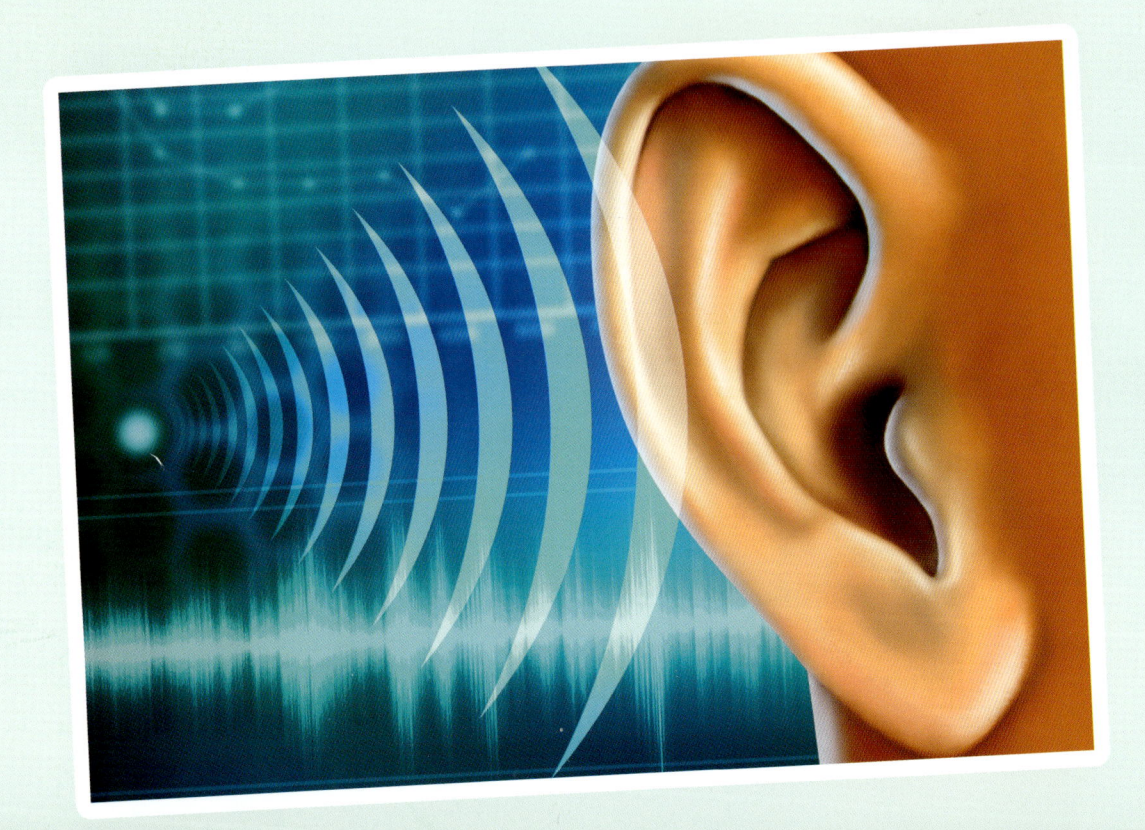

eardrum

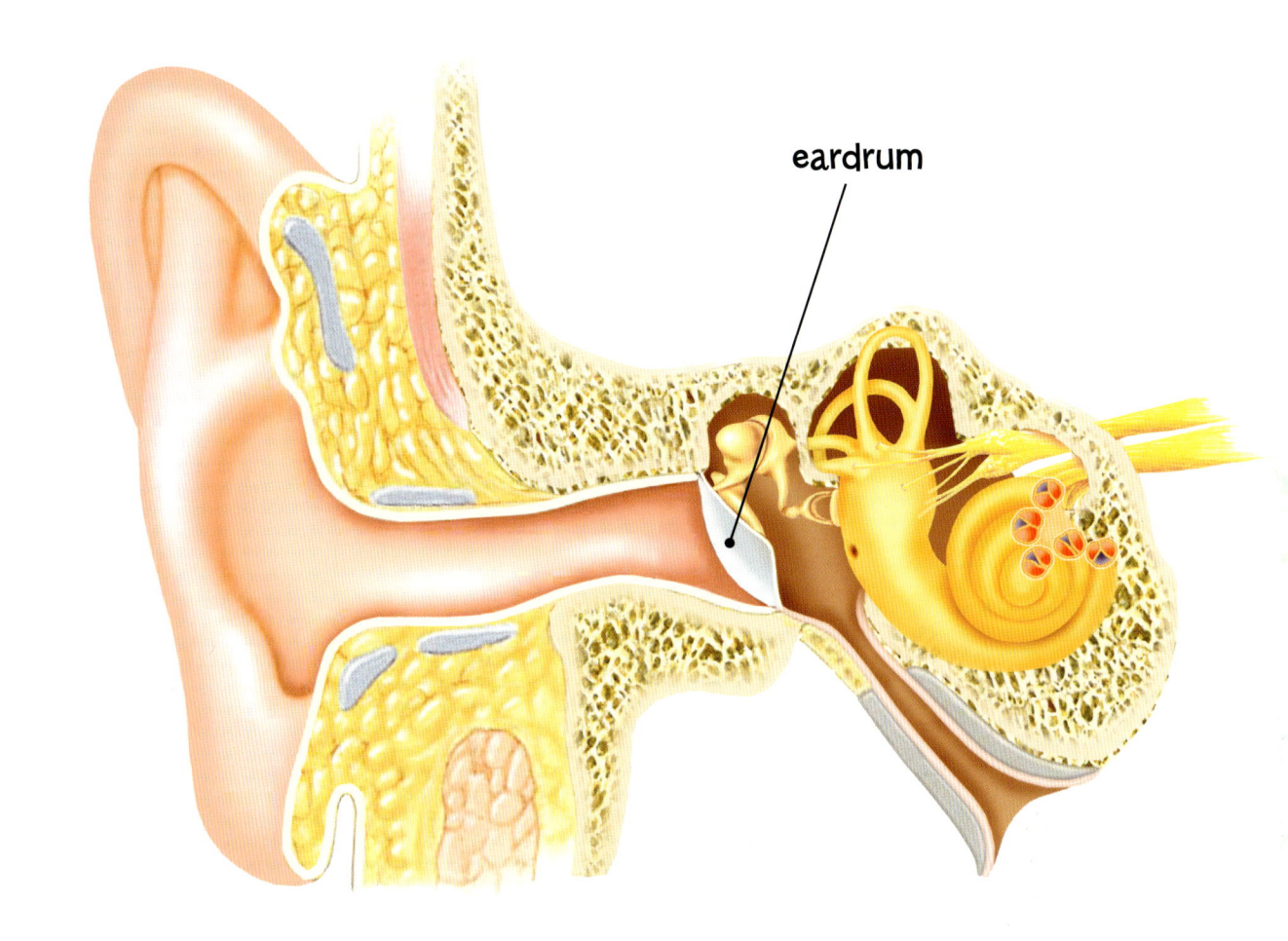

The **eardrum** is deep inside your ear. The moving sound wave touches the eardrum. The eardrum starts to move back and forth. The eardrum vibrates.

SOUND MESSAGES

When your eardrum vibrates, it sends a message to your brain. Your brain tells you what the sound is. Sounds can be loud like a balloon popping or soft like a whisper.

You brain can tell where the sound is. When a dog barks, you don't have to see the dog to know where it is. Your brain tells you.

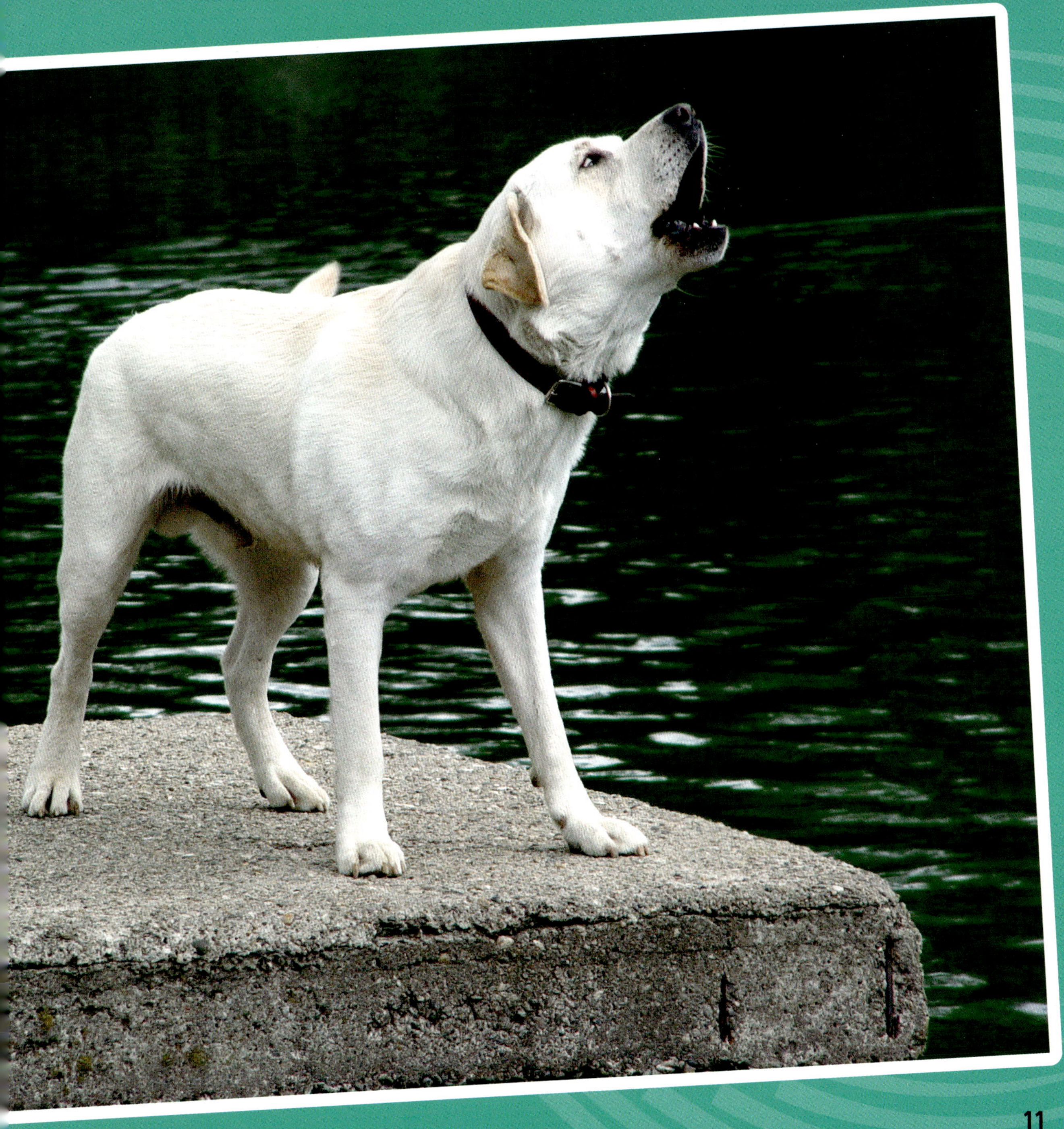

PITCH

Remember the moving rubber band? A thin band will make a high sound. A thicker band will make a low sound. **Pitch** is the highness or lowness of a sound.

A whistle makes a high sound. A rumble of thunder is a low sound. Listen to a bird sing. Listen to a dog growl. Which sound is high? Which sound is low?

ECHO

Sound can bounce. When sound waves hit something hard, they bounce back.

reflected wave

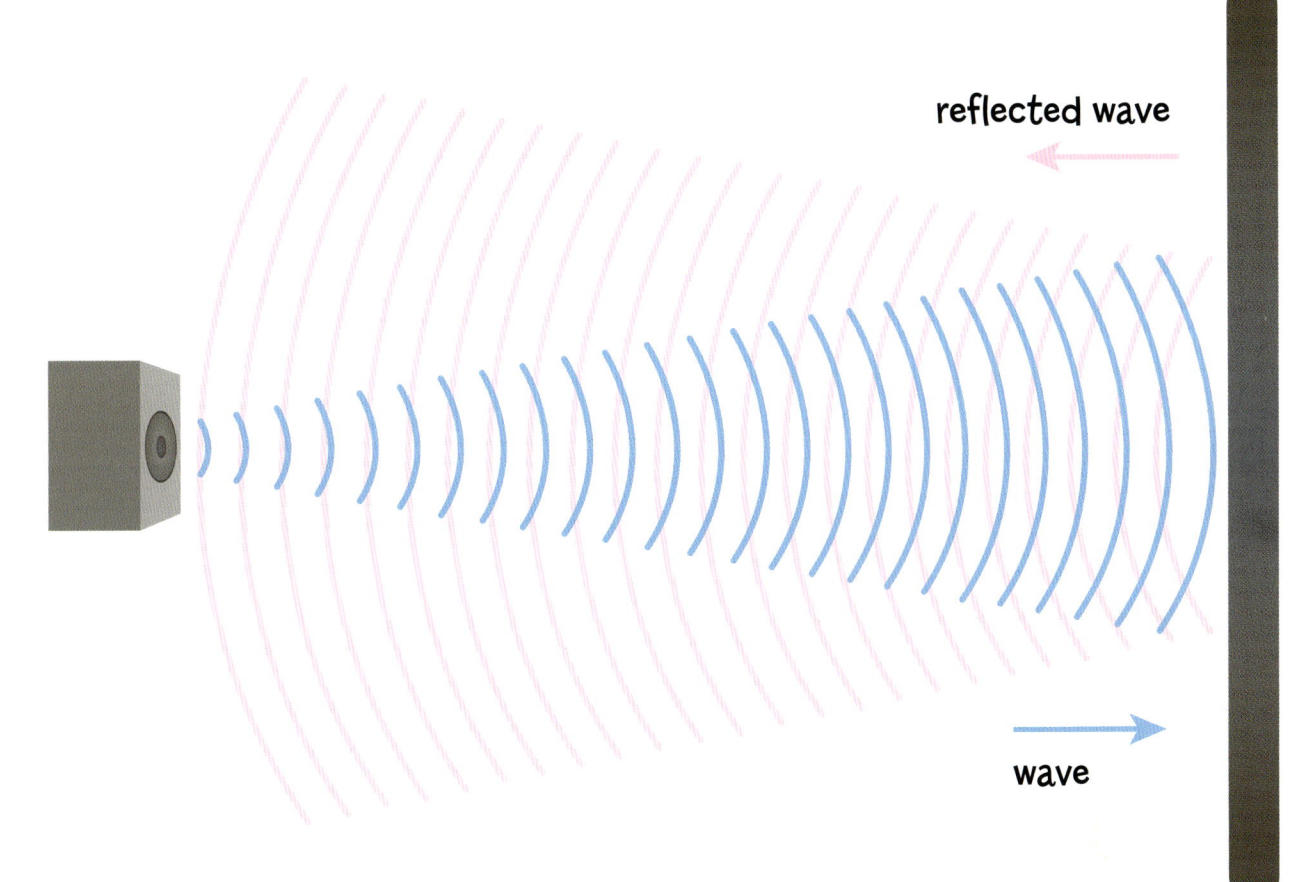

wave

Shout "hello" in an empty room. Sound waves leave your mouth and hit the walls. The waves bounce back fast. You may hear the word again. This is called an **echo**.

Bats use bouncing waves to help them fly. Bats can't see very well. But they have very good ears.

The bat calls out. The sound wave moves fast. The wave hits a tree. The sound bounces back. The bat hears the echo. This tells the bat that something is in its way. Now the bat can safely fly around the tree.

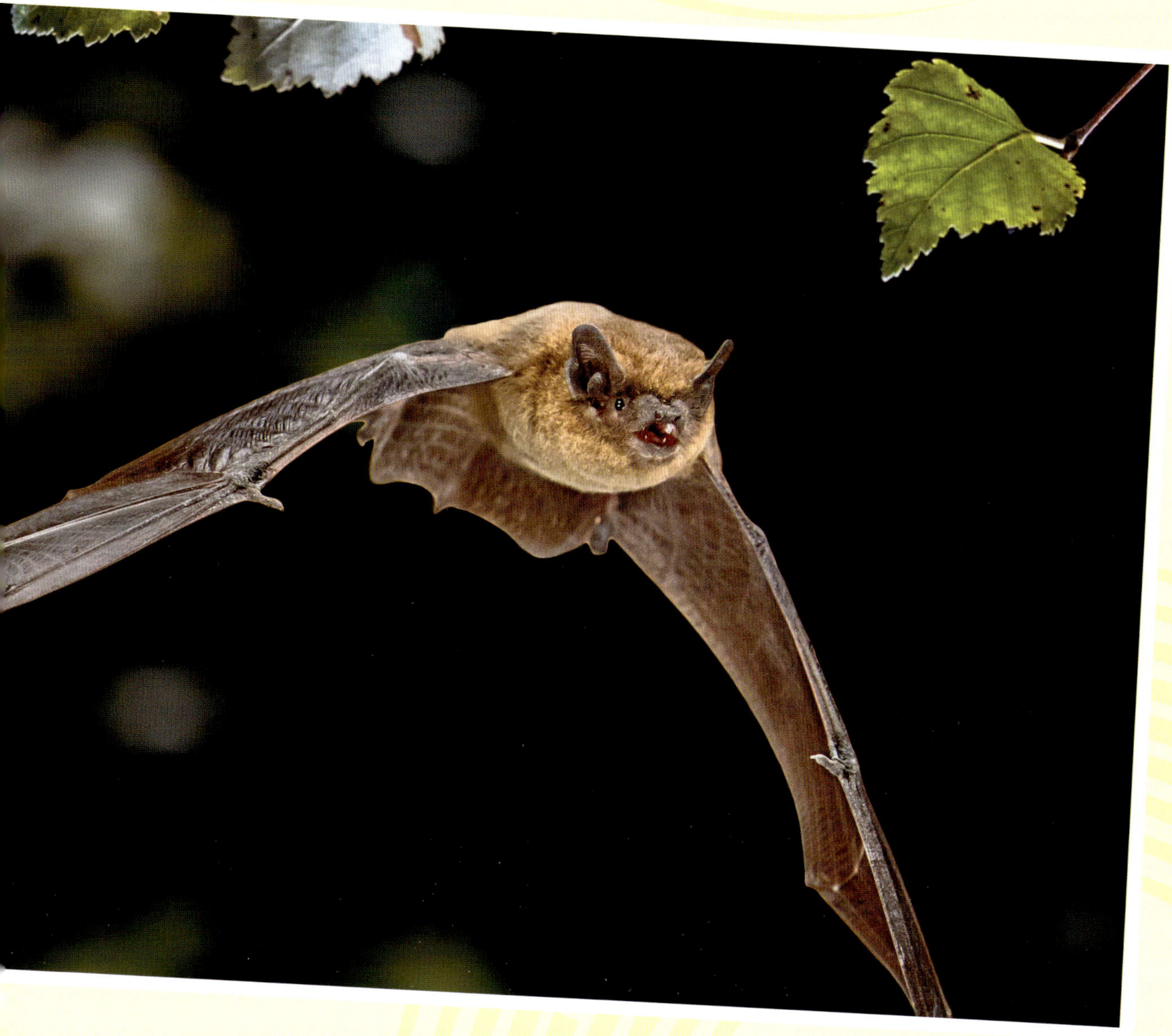

SOUND ALL AROUND

Sound tells us information. We know school is starting when we hear the school bell. We know a fire engine is coming when we hear its siren.

When you finish this book, make a sound. Close the book's cover slowly. Make a quiet sound. Shhhhhhhh!

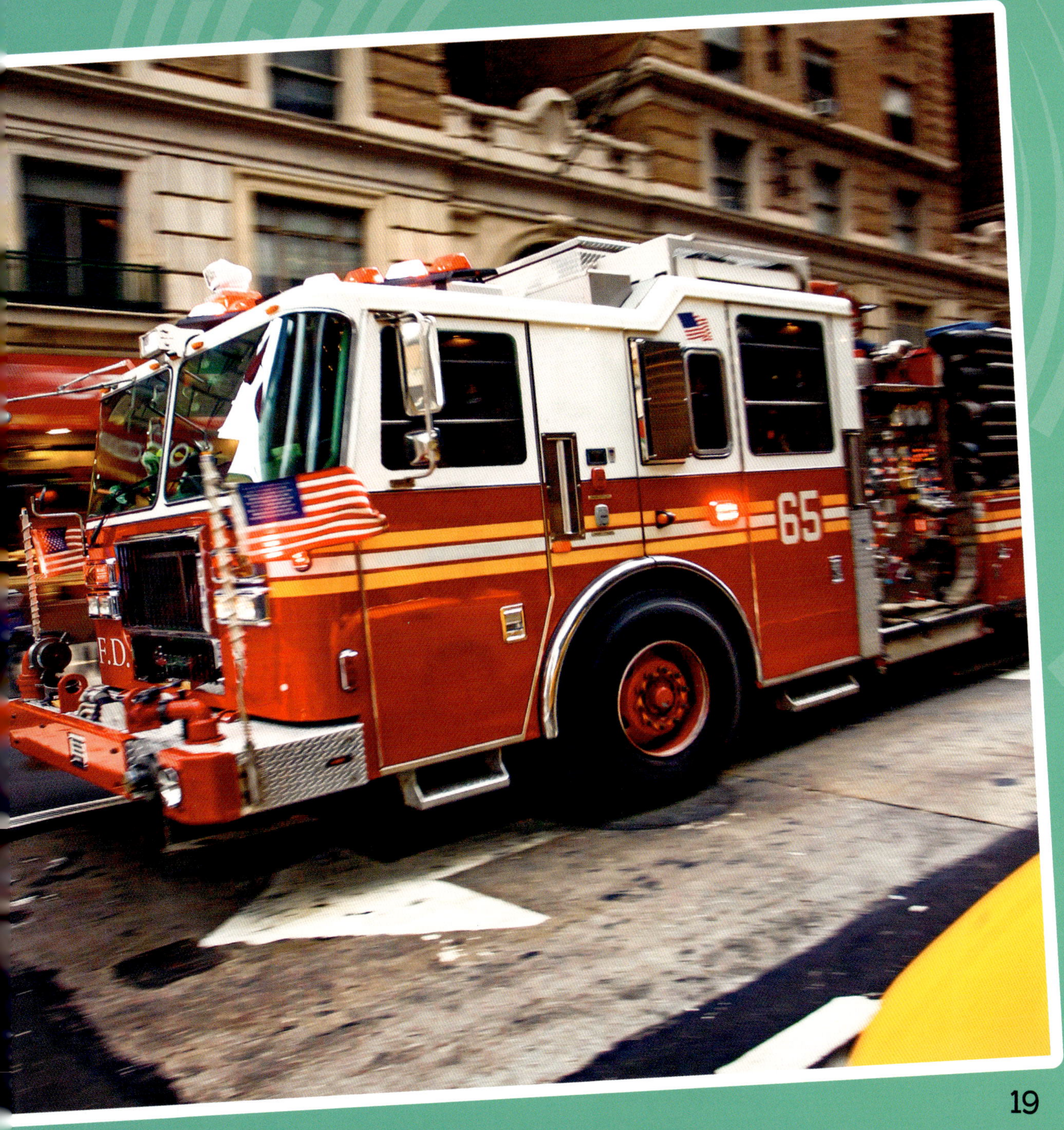
65
F.D.

MAKE MUSICAL SOUND WAVES

Find out if different amounts of water make different sounds.

What you need:
- three or four water glasses (made of glass)
- a metal spoon

What you do:

1. Place the glasses in a line.
2. Fill the glasses with different amounts of water.
3. Use a metal spoon to gently tap the side of each glass.
4. Listen carefully.

Can you hear a different pitch from each glass? Are some sounds higher or lower than others?

Change the water amount in the glasses. Does that change the pitch? Why or why not?

GLOSSARY

eardrum a part of your ear that helps you hear sound waves

echo a sound wave that bounces back to your ears

pitch how high or low a sound is

vibrate to move back and forth quickly

wave energy that moves through water or air

FIND OUT MORE

BOOKS

Experiments with Sound (Read and Experiment), Isabel Thomas (Raintree, 2015)

Sound (BOOM! Science), Georgia Amson-Bradshaw (Wayland, 2019)

Sound (Little Physicist), Megan Cooley Peterson (Raintree, 2020)

WEBSITES

Sound

www.dkfindout.com/us/science/sound/

What are sound waves? BBC Bitesize

www.bbc.co.uk/bitesize/topics/zw982hv/articles/z8mmb82

INDEX

air 4, 6

bats 16

brain 10

eardrums 9, 10

ears 4, 8, 9

echoes 15, 16

hearing 4, 6, 8, 10, 15, 18

loud sounds 10

pitch 12

soft sounds 10

sound waves 4, 6, 8, 9, 10, 14, 15, 16, 18

vibrating 6, 9, 10